8 MINUTE DECISION

8 minutes all it takes to change Your life

Rastogi *Siddhartha*

ISBN : 978-93-85818-66-0

Thanks Dad for being with me always

Summary

*I*t's an interesting read for everybody who is doing something or nothing in life. Anybody who is confused, who is looking for answers, or blocked with no thoughts, no options or somebody who has multiple options. Every believer or non-believer would find value from this book.

This book is about decision making and its linkage with your success in life irrespective of matter in consideration which can be love, money, power, friendship, business or fame etc.

Reading it a few times , especially going through the process of decision making would enable one to achieve high conviction and higher probability of deriving success from the methodology devised.

Some examples in this book have been given using male gender but these examples are applicable for women folk as well. No sex or gender bias exists whilst writing or practicing this book. Some views and comments have been made on the political scenario and situation which might not necessarily conform your views of the situation.

This is a short and concise book. **_But there are three methods to read it._** First, you can read the book like a novel or a story book and learn the theory & practice of *"TRI -O-MPH"*. Second, read Chapter 1 & 3 and straight move to the last two chapters- *TPH methodology*. Third, read the title and head to the last eight pages of the book. Each reading would have different outcome. Choose as per your style and time you have.

First method, would take you through the spiritual and scientific path of decision making and would bring clarity in your mind on how easy and promptly you can change your path and be a winner, helping you to achieve wealth, success, fame and results which you have always longed for. It also substantiates the process of doing so, reasoning and questions which constantly hits your mind.

Second method will straight answer your questions and push you right away to take action, follow the process and derive the result quickly.

The third one would straight lead you to the process to generate desired outcome.

The key thing before following any of these methods is to have an open mind which is looking for answers and is willing to adapt. A closed mind with a huge baggage stuffed with years of experience would only make this reading redundant for you and thus you trashing the most important process which you are about to learn........

How can you open your mind to read this book?
Simply take eight deep long breaths and tell yourself, your heart, your mind, that I'm open to learning, open to make the right decision and open to change my life and be a winner.

Contents

First let's connect and understand each other !!!!!

efore I start the content of the book, let me first thank you for having picked up this book for reading. I 'm like you who is reading this book and wondering what I can gain from this book. Happiness, knowledge, thrill, excitement, sadness or just that I don't have any other work and hence I' m reading this book. One thing I can assure you that language of this book is simple and straight forward and would help you in taking decisions which are right or would prove right in the years to come by in your life. Important objective of this book is to bring the focus back on you, your inner power to decide, your strengths, your decisions which will impact you positively.

This book is about to transform your life through effective decision making. Decision making is a complex mix of science and art, which draws power from the individual in question forcing him or her to bring harmony with oneself and propel the individual to move forward. It's a form of science as it's driven by facts, figures and objectives which you can see and feel whilst a lot or most of it is art as it's powered and directed by Universal goals and Omens.

This book has been written with pointers having multiple chapters for decision makers to take a pause on their reading and practice what they have just read.

The best methodology to extract most out of this book is to read every question twice and see its relevance in day today life and on past decisions one has taken till now, while moving forward in his or her journey. Also it's important that the reader closes the book, shuts his eyes and visualizes the last major or important decision he or she has taken in his or her life. Reader has to put these chapters in perspective of his or her last decision and at the end of all eight steps, see if the decision taken by him or her would have been different. If the answer comes as affirmative in that case, reader should take a step further to see the changes the correct decision would have brought in life at that point in time and in turn to his or her present life. Also it's relevant from the perspective that defines, "***What went behind that decision making and what must be avoided in future for taking decisions***".

In this book, examples have been given of some very close family members and their influence on the decisions taken by you. Quite a few of them might sound disagreeable in first go, but when you ponder on all what has been guided to you, through the years and what has been the outcome, a clear picture as serene as night dew would emerge in front of you. Idea of such examples is to allow you to connect **You,** with what has happened in the past and what **should not happen** in future. Until one realizes the wrongs and ills, the definition of right and correct doesn't form picture in one's mind. There is bad and hence there is good in life. There is devil and hence God exists, there is confusion, irritation and unhappiness and hence there exists the concept of peace.

Some of the texts in this book are repeated in different forms and different language. This is to make sure that you understand and imbibe the context in which it's being presented and take right view of that.

Part of this book will make you feel agitated and angry with yourself. But focus of the book remains the future decision which will come your way and can improve your future life.

You may have heard of a famous saying, "It's all good to say or easy to say on the hindsight, but that didn't happen". Question comes back again why it didn't happen, because the decision taken was different and till then there was nobody to guide you to take the correct one.

If you consolidate most decisions you have taken till now, one simple fact would emerge, that *you are a victim of your smart mind. What we believe our mind has comprehended is right for us with using our inner conscience which is pure and is currently contaminated by our own process of denial which we have harnessed by satiating and fulfilling our various emotions.*

Most of us are unaware of what lies ahead of us. We use astrologers, palmists and other fortune tellers and their methodologies. Sometimes we define our future and goals of our loved ones by the sermons and outcome of such predictions. If I take a decision which is contrary to what I actually believe and then approach any fortune teller, it would be impossible for him to do a course correction.

For each one of us, Life is nothing but a collection of decisions. Lots of us believe that what happens to us is because of our destiny or what was fated to be. But if you look back and analyze, fate or destiny was instrumental in bringing you choices at your door step and what decision you took years back either made you climb heights of success or made you languish. We believe that the right thing happens at right place. But if you don't take the decision to pursue the opportunity, how would you move forward.

No one has a crystal maze which can tell you what is it that one should do? We don't know the bigger picture. Universe knows it. Universe has the complete plan of what will happen in future or atleast has the knowledge of it.

Sometimes, we rely on our intuition, gut, feel.

What do all these reflect?

These are nothing but indicators or cues through which Universe is hinting us.

Why did these come to us?

These came to us because; we were one with the Universe. We believed that Universe would guide us the right path which is beneficial for Us first and **not harmful to others.** It's very important for us to know that each one of us deserves better and each one of us would get better. Point is at what cost. Price of betterment, cost or sacrifices have to be given by us. If we start using or exploiting others for our benefit, universal equilibrium gets lost and all indications given by universe ceases to come to us.

We all strive for more and extra. However, is it possible to keep getting more of one thing and not depleting other relevant things?

Universal equilibrium always needs to be maintained.

You work harder and you make more money, money comes and health goes. You work smarter, money comes your way but people's perception about you depletes. You earn more foes than friends. You suck up to your boss and you rise, you gain more money and better position, but you lose your credibility and become a spineless creature.

If you do ego massages of your clients' or superiors', your pride gets depleted.

When this planet earth was formed, all emotions were equal; the happiness one derived by playing with healthy children was as good at having a good season of crop. Having fun with friends in the rain was as good as achieving success in professional life. But then money came into existence. Everybody and everything started getting less importance than money.

If you have money, you are assumed to be happy. All emotions were scarified to gain monetary prowess.

But is it possible to make money, be happy, make the right decisions, not harm others and get universal help in achieving all what you desire. It is possible by enabling oneself to align with universe and get guidance in all acts and decisions.

We all have some similarities or atleast a few of them. We as humans never lose hope. We continue trying. We sometimes get caught up in our own routine and environmental cobweb through which we can't see and then in haste, confusion and zeal, then steps are taken which ruin our lives and lives of people whom we care and others around us. All of us have aspiration to do well for ourselves, better than what has been given to us or better than what we have experienced till now. *We want that our next day should bring more for us, compared to what we have already got.*

This journey or short sighted view leads us to take decisions which might result with superior returns and achievements in short run but can jeopardize our entire lives in long term.

Our lives like this World is in a state of imbalance or nonequilibrium. One side you have developed capitalist world that has surplus food, goods, amenities to live and on the other hand a continent in itself struggling to feed even 50% of its population, its people infected by deadly diseases and affected by natural calamities. A world where religion has taken a new meaning to achieve power, killing innocent women and children of the same religion in the name of religion.

Who are we to decide which religion the new born should adopt? Since we have adopted or our parents forced a religion on us, we assume that our offspring should also follow it and preach it. Then some people divide the religion further into sects, castes, sub castes, sub sects and follow age old processes, procedures, rituals and become the Power lords. They use religion as a means to gain strength. Every religion on this planet agrees to one thing, there is something beyond us which helps us and takes care of us when we require true almighty. Second we all love our children more than anything else. Our children look upto us for guidance and they don't understand what is good for them and heavily depend on us for their needs and affection and direction. Imagine these children whom we love the most have been sent by almighty or God through the process of birth and the same ones, we are killing or torturing to have a better life post our death or in this life, following old practices, gory practices) does that make any sense???

It clearly shows the men with stronger brain or I should say rigid brains are able to dominate us and manipulate us for their vested interests. Names can be anything, terrorists, anti-social elements etc. but the end result they are inflicting on the society is common. It's not that they don't have children or don't have heart or brains to think, but they have been either subjected to such disastrous experience or brainwashed, that they have forgotten the difference between ill and good. This book would help them to see within them, the good being and most importantly take decisions which are saner.

One day a friend asked me a question that what happens to people who come from poor backgrounds, from poor families with no skill set and no money to learn. My answer to her was people who come from poor or under privileged backgrounds are luckier than others since they don't come with any pressures or expectations. And as far as leaning is concerned, each one of us has a specific skillset. Every individual amongst the population of approx. 8.20 billion people, have some skillset. Some might have less of it, some might have more, but **all of us have something unique.** The question is whether we use that skill to portray ourselves to the world or we continue with our lives fighting with our environment and forgetting the natural skill almighty has gifted us. People who have used their skills, flourish to become legends and rest continue to only exist and survive.

Another thought, how should one realize what is Ones strength or one skill which can transform ones life completely. We are not born with a culture, language or religion but we surely born with a skill which is specific to us. And we need to know about it for us to excel in it. Once a friend who happens to be a corporate trainer told me that any individual with an average IQ *"Intelligence Quotient"* working on a job that involves a particular skill spends more than 10,000 man-hours, becomes the master of it. The same has been scientifically proven as well. Thus by working approx. four and half years, a man or woman can learn everything relevant to do any job or profession in this world. So, if you have skill and you know about it, how much simpler it would become then to excel and be an authority in that field. However important thing is you should enjoy what you are doing and be passionate about it.

We all have a role to play in this lifetime and if we become part of the Universal plan, our lives and lives of people we can influence can change significantly.

Human beings and only human beings on this planet have been given the power of choice. At any event, at any state, at any juncture we have multiple choices. If not multiple atleast two choices are present in front of us. These choices are neither bad nor good. Decisions which we take have repercussions. Some decisions have longer term impact on our lives whilst some have short term. Most of these decisions once taken can't be undone. Hence one needs to be sure what one is opting

16

for. Some of us are very careful and thus keep running away from taking any step or decision due to the fear of unknown. But one has to keep in mind that without taking concrete step to move in a direction, one can't progress.

In life if you are not progressing, you are stagnating.

A situation of status quo is a position of deceleration. Decision making is a very complicated process and that's what most people believe and thus try and capture all the possibilities involved. The environment around us is dynamic and hence one can never visualize all outcomes.

On an average, an individual takes 330 decisions in a day. Some of them are daily regular decisions which one has been taking for years. Past experiences of such decisions are well known and hence it easy to take such decisions quickly. Thus we take approximately 2300 decisions in a week or close to 10,000 in a month. In other words we are presented with almost 20,000 choices in a month. We make these choices and are mostly ignorant or callous or a non-believer of the outcome. We blame it all on Bhagwad Gita, where Lord Krishna stated ""not to worry or desire for the result but perform one's Karma or perform one's act"

But to perform Karma is also a decision. Now either you can choose to perform Karma or not to perform the act. What if the act is to harm somebody? Isn't it better in such a case to avoid that act all together than performing it? Context of Bhagwad Gita is relevant, when the decision has been taken to finish the evil thereby bringing peace and harmony back in this world.

Every month out of 10,000 decisions we take, there are roughly four to five occasions which are not routine. These are the decisions in our lives for which we have no prior experience of end result. Neither have we experienced it before nor have we seen any near or dear ones living with it. So now the question arises how should we decide?

I started my day early today, it was a bright sunny Tuesday morning. I was not expecting rush and crowded roads to work. Unfortunately the road I take usually, was blocked since a tree had fallen and hence the traffic needed to be diverted. I reached office at the nick of time for the weekly conference call to start. My stomach was growling and I was very hungry. I knew that if I skip my first meal, I would get a severe migraine attack. And then I would have to pop some pills. Unfortunately my boss is not aware of how my body would react to this peculiar situation. Now I have

18

to take a few decisions. First whether I should go to the cafeteria or dutifully go to the conference room where the call has been initiated where I am expected to be present. Once I take this major decision, many more will come my way. If I go to the cafeteria, what should I tell my boss? Should I tell him the truth and complete truth, series of events which happened in the morning or should I give some lame excuse like somebody in the family fell sick etc. In case I decide to go directly to the conference hall, should I inform my superior of my situation in brief or just sit through the call. Alternatively, I can decide to the conference hall and give my boss another excuse of a client actionable to be done and under that pretext visit the cafeteria and finish my breakfast. Multiple decisions, but broadly two outcomes. First one is to suffer a migraine attack and second one is no migraine. But with all choices I have made, repercussions would be very different for the all five versions stated above. The boss would definitely have more discomforting discussions post the call is over. Hence neither I would be at peace nor would he be. My motivation levels would be down and my focus on work would reduce. Gradually I would start looking out for opportunities outside my company and would move out for wrong reasons or non-issues rather that right ones.

What if somebody would have guided me to take next steps which would be beneficial to me and would lead to only positive outcome and continued harmony between me and my boss?

And who in this world has the best idea of the situation. Who knows what's the best for me, knows what will yield me maximum benefit in any good or sticky situation. **There is only person and that's ME.** I know which the best decision for me is. I know the situation and I know how it can be tackled in the best possible way keeping all the variables in sync with the environment yielding desirable results from **MY perspective**.

Isn't it interesting that I'm the one who is deciding , I'm the one who is not control and I'm the one who is not sure and I'm the one who has doubts and finally the fauxpas happens.

What if there is a process of helping me take right decisions. **8 minutes** process which can lead me to the path which will only bring me good. A technique, a process which is evolutionary.

When one right decision is taken amongst so many average decisions, life turns complete 360 degrees. Riches come towards you and it happens so quickly and in such abundance, that you feel where it has been hiding all through these years of you chasing it.

When you are in sync with the decision you have taken, in other words, your mind and body only knows about that decision thereby forgetting the rest. Success of such decision is inevitable. How when you enter a new five star hotel and you visit the bathroom. So many knobs and buttons exists spraying water from all sides and suddenly one press of button and hot water gushes out with full force, what you have been looking for last ten minutes.

All you need is one right decision to work for you, and all your needs, financial, emotional would be taken care of. One decision amongst so many of them which in itself is not going to be presented to you until you are ready for it. You will see, going forward, how the right decision is the last step. First are the choices that appear before the decision is taken and are you ready to face the options and choices. You have to be prepared to embrace that change which would come post the decision is taken. That decision would ask for your commitment, for your time, for all you have because journey post that decision would never be the same again. It would make you successful, rich, famous, happy, social, popular, renowned, respected, what you have longed for all these years.

Most people around the world, have the habit of escaping from decisions. Issues which people feel while taking them can be one or more amongst many jotted down here.

Fear of what if?

Fear of decision going wrong,

Can I defend my decision if anyone asks about it? ,

How can I take this decision?

Do I have the authority to take it?

Do I have the understanding to take this decision?

It doesn't come in my purview.

What benefit I would after I take this decision?

Who would follow next steps after taking the decision?

Does this give me some immediate benefit?

In long term, we all are dead so why take this decision which would make relevance after few years?

What would others think of me if I take this decision?

And many such question which only confuses ones mind and shows the unpreparedness of taking the plunge and conquering success. It's most likely that people who lead ordinary lives, cribbing about everything in life, when presented with an opportunity would give a pass if it comes in a disguised form through a strong decision.

The biggest challenge lies for the people who have come up to middle class and upper middle. For them the thought of losing what you have achieved in social and monetary terms keeps them away from taking any decision. At the same time, most of the poor and underprivileged lot is so engrossed in the routine rut from work to stomach and back, that they ignore the opportunities around them. Rich encash it by allocating some resources and taking marginal benefits. But one who doesn't believe in going all out, will never get the decision completely right. Wars have been won by men who don't think of their people back home but by those who see the head of the enemy as the only prize to have ever achieved.

Chapter 1:

Our Life: Sum of Equal Parts

Our lives are divided into four parts. On an average every alternate part would witness highs and lows. For example if you had a great and loving childhood, your adolescent age till mid-thirties would not be so enjoyable and then your peak period would arrive having generally a better time than the previous one. In a nutshell, these four phases of peaks and troughs would be witnessed by each individual during their life time. If you sit back and relax, closing your eyes and step outside your body as if you are watching your life as a movie. Starting from the first memory of winning , to the first gift you got, run the reel of life at a fast pace and you would realise those times when you really had good happy periods and a few years when you were generally not happy, being or doing what you have been. This is a natural cycle and each one coming on this planet has to go through this irrespective of the stature, money, position, power etc.

However, what is important in this journey of life is to reduce the unhappiness, worries, sadness, irritation,

24

confrontation during those generic periods which have arrived after years of happiness.

What can I do to bring that change?

How can it be altered, when I'm destined to go through it?

Is it universally applicable? What if this theory won't impact me?

We human beings have been given a unique power from the time we are born. **The power to decide.** This power is not given to other co inhabitants of this planet. Right decisions can change everything in our life. It can shape our destiny, it can alleviate us from the problems which we are currently facing or may potentially face in future. It's applicable in every one's life and hits each one of us someday.

In life there are three instances where this theory of right decision holds extreme importance and great value. On an overall basis, you would experience constant need of taking decision and pursuing your dreams to achieve success in your life. But little do you realize that decisions if taken casually would be irreversible and repercussions and outcome of such choices can keep hitting you much later in your life even when you have forgotten about those decisions.

Hence it's critical that choices, options which are presented in front of you or which cross your path should be evaluated and considered *without any biases or prejudices* <u>*strictly overlooking past experiences*</u> of people and hearsay from those, who might have been relevant in your entire life till now or have been relevant at some point in time.

As mentioned earlier, life is divided into parts & phases, but there are three instances, which generally mark the periods of change from general well being or sadness to attaining a state of real happiness and ecstasy and vice versa.

First stage arrives in your life, when you are in your mid-teens, studying in high school, preparing for secondary school examination or have given one just now, hormonal changes are on the rise and you are oblivious about it. Your family is concerned about you and your future, but has limited options at their disposal to guide you and hand hold you. Your energy levels are very high. You feel you can achieve anything in this world. Everything seems doable. Moral conflicts and rules laid down by the society come your way to act and practice free spirit. You follow and observe multiple icons and successful people but are still confused about your life goal. You see the topper of your batch or your best friend making a certain choice and he has been perceived as the smartest kid by everyone in the school, hence you choose to follow him and pursue what he is doing. Or perhaps your dad has been successful in his job or his profession and you are his son or daughter, thus it is taken for granted that you would continue to take the legacy forward and follow his path. Also it seems like a safe and an easy route. You evaluate and ponder that even if you fail, you can blame parents that they forced you to get into it. Even if you are a mediocre in that field, your father's business or profession, contacts, influence etc. exists for you to carry it forward. After all he has so many years of experience, so whatever he is suggesting is correct and right for you.

Whilst your next steps in your professional life or career are being decided jointly by family, relatives and social committee, you have started experiencing something on personal front as well. You want to look smart and dashing not for yourself but to impress everyone around. At this stage you are infatuated with a girl whom you have just seen and you expect her to have similar feelings for you. Or you are already dating someone for past two years and now she is going abroad to study. You always thought she is your soulmate and you would marry her and be with her always. What now?

27

Just yesterday another girl said hello to you outside the cafeteria. Is she the one you were long looking for all through these years? You want to feel her, you want to know what is she like. But what happens to the one you have been dating. "But isn't she going anyways out of my life."

Your father wants you to go abroad and study but all friends are here and anyways Uncle who came from Europe said that, "Outside India, it's bad, economy is failing, so why should I go??"

Second instance in your life would come when you are in your late thirties and very early forties. At this stage, you are mostly married with kids and you are experiencing lack of family affection, mainly from your spouse. You have a tough business or even tougher job to execute on a day today basis and above all this, expectations from the family is just mounting up. You want to do something more, something different but don't have the time, energy and most significant is your indecisiveness which is holding you back. Is it the right thing to do? You followed your family tradition and pursued the profession or business your father, grandfather had been pursuing or at times, you just keep following what others told you to do. You never decided to have banking as your profession, apologies, not a banker, banker is a dignified word. You have become a sales agent who is just running after daily numbers. Wow, when is the next promotion, you would manage some of these bankers, not again, not these bankers but sales agents pushing various products under the garb of asset allocation, advisory portfolio, financial planning, tax saving, retirement planning, goal achievement etc. etc.

No, no you are not a retail banker, not a mutual fund agent, not an insurance agent, not a small and medium enterprise advisor but you are an investment banker doing big deals, only executing fund raising transactions from public markets and advising on large mergers and acquisitions. You travel almost half the world every fortnight and stay in the swankiest five star hotels. Obviously all on company account or on client account as you are the expert. (*I always wondered why rich people, rich professionals, and rich businessmen take advice from advisors, bankers thinking as if they are experts in their field. If that would have been the case, all advisors would have been billionaires; obviously that's not the case. That's a different topic we would touch in other book.*) This is what you always wanted to do in life and you have achieved everything in life now. Your wife socializes with the who's who of the society and your kids go to an international school, and the school fee that you pay in a year is obviously more than what you have paid for entire fifteen years of your education. You have got everything but still there is so much fatigue. Despite of these luxuries and success, there is a void. Something is missing and you can feel it. You miss holding your kids and playing with them. Anyhow they attend so many classes (extra ones, so that they become smart), that they don't have time for you. Your wife is busy with her social circle and her set of friends. You went to the best engineering college, struggled hard to get in there and then the best B – School. You felt that by attending these schools you would not only make money but also innovate, do something bigger and more meaningful in life. You want to do more for the society but then where is the time? How would you earn this kind of money, if you give up your job, your profession for a social cause, which you strongly believe in? You have been donating money and that's enough? You party every night, meet same old friends and have fun. But thought of "being meaningless" keeps haunting you again and again...

Third instance would hit your life, when you are in your mid-fifties. Your children have been growing up well and they have a life of their own. You have achieved professional success, you have wealth to sustain yourself and you are busy managing it. You are taking life relatively easy, but something interesting has come your way. Are you going to take that plunge? "Is it going to be beneficial for me? Is it going to provide me with the success, happiness peace of mind which I have been looking for years? Or is it just another web in which I will get entangled?"

One good news of life is, life constantly keeps presenting you with opportunities what you are and what you want to be. You give up on life, on yourself, but life doesn't and hence life's constant endeavor is to push you do what you are good at, what can add value to you, what you can add back to the world and what would make you happy and satisfied. If one believes in rebirth, life today and always constantly presents you to achieve whatever you have longed for and without the need for you to come back on this worldly platform again. Life helps you achieve emancipation or moksha or *Mukti.*

The first important choice or decision which is presented in front of you is generally at the age between 15 to 18 years. Decision taken by you at that time out of social, emotional or economic sensibilities would seem right to you. This decision could have been guided by strong influencers and intelligent people in your life. You think that this is the path and hence you would persevere to achieve success. With hard work and intelligence work combined with diplomatic and social skills you would feel like a winner and an achiever by the time you are 26 to 28 years old. But quest for something more, something different is still there. As you are enjoying your success and victory and your restless search for the next, you would be presented another opportunity. Perhaps this time you are not so lucky. In another 8 to 10 years, by the time you turn 34 to 36, you realize you are heading nowhere. Don't worry, another life changing opportunity is about to come in your life and another one by 44 to 46 and one more by 52 to 54 and the last one from 62 to 64.

At these instances of your life one right decision would take you to the next level of success and achievement as you have the power today to change the world. Many more such occasions would hit you your life, every now and then when you feel the need to decide and want to be on the right path and this book would assist you in achieving that route which would lead you to _**Your meaning of Success.**_ This book would lead your path, would assist you to choose, to decide and have a course correction if needed and make you achieve and win what you have been longing for all these years.

Chapter 2
Ariso decision makers - ArisoDs

*I*n 2015, terrorism saw its worst outcome. What started three decades back, an endeavor from Russia to dominate the West Asian region has destabilized the entire Middle Eastern geography? US entered the conflict indirectly by creating and giving support to religious fundamentalist militia which in later years has posed threat to its own country. Parallel to this, US created a new conflict zone in Iraq to prove it's supremacy on the world overthrowing the Iraqi regime of Sadaam Hussein thus leaving Iraqi region and Iraqi people in a worse off situation than. *Every wrong decision in the world by a human being or by a world leader leads to a downward spiral making society worse off than before.* This holds true for lesser known mortals as well. Conflict in Iraq not only shook the economy, but killed millions of innocent people who had to face atrocities worse than death. In many cases, death took away pain inflicted upon them. Conflict also engulfed the nearby region of Syria expanding its vicious expanse.

During this uncertainty, a well thought out long term beneficial decision was taken....

Who took this decision??

What was that decision??

Was it a right decision??

What can be its long term repercussions??

Angela Merkel, the German chancellor, "2015 Time Person of Year" took a call to allow millions of conflict affected, terrorism hit people to seek asylum in Germany and pressurizing other European nations to do the same. Displaced people now had a hope of a good future and prospective social security. What has this decision done to Germany and other European nations? It has added more than a million hands and mouths. Europe which has been suffering from the burden of aging population has now suddenly got large number of young refugees who are willing to work at very low wages, thereby increasing the productivity of the country as well as fueling domestic consumption. Short term social unrest is bound to happen till they gel well in the European socio economic system, in the same way as sugar mixes with milk making the milk sweeter losing its own existence all together.

How did Angela Merkel take this decision despite of being fully aware that she would meet resistance on this decision from her own team and obviously from critics? Subsequent pages of this book can help to describe the phenomenon of long term beneficial decisions.

China, in last decade and a half has emerged as the single growth engine of the world. Economics and politics revolved around Chinese communist party's endeavor to evolve as the world's largest superpower. But one man's decision has changed everything. One man who decided to oppose the suppressive rule of Chinese in Hongkong. Joshua Wong Chi fung, one of the youngest individuals to mobilize millions of people and get their support to fight the mighty Chinese Communist regime. A person with dyslexic learning capabilities achieved and continues to influence millions in their hope to have more autonomy in Hongkong away from the autocratic grip of Chinese. One man who led the umbrella revolution in HongKong decided to push for more political rights and democratic options to the fellow beings in Hongkong.

Andre Agassi, the leading tennis player, who hated to play tennis but due to his decision to be number one in the world, emerged as the oldest player to conquer the title. At the age of thirty three and a half when most tennis players either retire or take coaching as their profession, Andre Agassi became the number One player as per ATP rankings.

Many more examples like Jack Ma, Mahatma Gandhi Abraham Lincoln, Nelson Mandela, Bill Gates, Steve Jobs, Mother Teresa, Margret Thatcher have taken a decision which changed not only the path of their lives but brought the world into a new era.

One right decision followed by several others and more and many more and their names will remain till human history is written and rewritten.

How have these men & women from ordinary humble background and ordinary knowledge achieve these heights of success. One decision which worked for them and that's all it takes for one to become the greatest.

How did these great people arrive at this decision or concluded to take the path which ultimately led them to glory.

Is it luck? Is it smartness or Providence helped them? Honest answer is nobody knows. Some or most of them would have followed the decision making process as has been laid down in later chapters of the book. Perhaps yes. But these Ariso Ds have one thing in common, they have been chosen by the Universe to change the destiny and journey of this planet.

Are you the chosen one as well?
How would you know?

Perhaps you are the one but you will never be able to follow the path Providence and Universe has chosen for you. Perhaps you were so close to it that one right move and you would have been in a different trajectory and a different league.

Not everybody is as lucky that right decisions are just inflicted upon them. Not everyone is destiny's child but that doesn't make you less suitable to achieve heights of financial and social success. Thus for people who can't find the path , who are unsure of the journey ahead this book would guide them as candle light through dark forests of uncertainty and hopelessness.

Every human being seeks for three things – Love, Money & Power not in specific order but necessarily either of them and eventually all of them. How to decide, which one to follow first and which one would lead to other and its route.

How do we usually decide?

It's either out of fear or out of too much of enthusiasm or out to prove a point.

Is it the right way?

If not, what is the right path?

People who have mastered the art of decision making have followed few or more principles of this book and hence have reached heights of success.

I am the decision maker of my own fortune.

Let's start with the *TRI- O- UMPH Technique*

Chapter- 3
T - Trim the tumult & Cut the Noise

The most important step to sense what is good for us and in order to take a step towards right decision making is to cut the noise and trim the commotion around you. Has it ever happened to you? You are sitting in a sales review and your boss is giving you a lecture and talking about targets, you are trying to be attentive and then all of a sudden you don't hear anything. You are physically there in that room attending every moment but still you can't experience anything. It sometime happens in meetings. Somebody has come to meet you and he is explaining and talking but you are not there. It generally happens out of exhaustion or fatigue. But imagine if you have a mental ON & OFF Switch which can allow you to take in or stop as and when you desire. We all already have that switch with us and within us. It only needs to get activated. System is already inbuilt within us, we have to figure out its mode of working. Let's understand how we can do it.

There are generally Six major emotions we experience.

Fear - feeling afraid or being terrorized or shock or phobia.

Anger - feeling angry or getting raged .

Sadness - sorrow, grief (a stronger feeling, for example when someone has died) or depression (feeling sad for a long time). Some people think depression is a different emotion.

Joy - feeling happy. Other words are happiness, gladness.

Disgust - feeling something is wrong or dirty

Trust - a positive emotion; admiration is stronger; acceptance is weaker.

Out of these 6 major emotions, if one is able to manage single emotion of Fear, Noise plug can be activated.

Fear can be of different kinds. Examination fear, performance fear, delivery fear, outcome fear, rejection fear, supernatural fear, fear from certain things, fear of certain people or certain places or certain situations.

A child is born with no fear and no guilt. Hence it's only appropriate to state that fear has been acquired by us during our journey of life. Some negative thoughts have mastered our brain and that sometimes, can be due to reasons beyond our control. It could have happened due to parents focusing more on our siblings, abusive parents, abusive teachers, notions created by adult behavior in our lives or some explanations given to us since our childhood.

Sometimes, when the child is not hungry and parents wish to feed the child, they say, eat else, Dracula, ghost or some deadly power would come and would take him away. In the mind of the child, he is associating his not eating, as a behavior which would lead to evil company and he starts developing phobia for it.

Some people stammer or some people can't talk or deliver speech in public forums. Most of them may have been laughed at or joked about during early part of their lives, when they delivered their first performance. Conception of that negative thought becomes even stronger over the years.

All phobias, low confidence, fear of not coming back, life not taking shape have deep connection with our lives influencers. Yesterday, I read an article about a boy from Hyderabad, India belonging to a well to do family studying MSc in Computer Science from one of the prestigious universities in US committing suicide. A boy who had no problem of money, who was one of the highest graders of India's premier institute IIT – Chennai and then studying further to earn more, achieve more, commits suicide just because he got low grades in one of terms. Something within him was programmed erroneously.

He was aware and well informed but never questioned the beliefs, rituals and life objectives which were taught to him. We all have strong influencers in our lives. It keeps changing every ten to twelve years. In our lives roughly three people play a major role in shaping our thoughts and beliefs. And if that influencer equates high marks as sign of success, we start believing it. Repercussions can be, any set back in life and we believe that life is over. It's finished. It's only because we have heard way too much, listened too much without questioning. We have not paid heed to our experience, logic, intuitions and omens around us. Thus the first step in moving towards the decision making which will be in sync with the Universe is to cut the advice, verbal help, and suggestions from our so called well-wishers.

Some of them have gone through what we are going through and some of them by method of estimation come with a perspective and believe that their advice or some time, their views which have now become rigid rules, is the right way to operate. A set of twins given same care turn out to be different natured individuals with different wants, different views, different inner desires and social requirements. Then how can people in different scenarios and different surroundings be guided or forced in a single way which the one advising believes, would lead to success.

As pointed out earlier, in your life atleast three and atmost five people have maximum influence who impacts oneself. Important point to note is that none of these five people nor their advice plays a role beyond three to five percent in shaping our future or changing our present. Generally the first influencer in our lives are our parents or siblings in case the child is not the first one to be born in the family and age difference between parents and the child is significantly higher. In some case cases where abusive families don't give affection to the child, influencer can be foster parents or teachers or caretaker. Now let's take three scenarios. A child born to rich parents, high class society business family. Child is taken good care by nanny or maid. Parents' intervention is minimal in the upbringing, in case the mother of the child is also working. Child is more emotionally dependent on grand parents or nanny for emotional wellbeing and seeking worldly perspectives. Now imagine, Nanny or grandparents advising on matters pertaining to current world which is ever changing who have their idiosyncrasies and social and economic background. Parents on the other hand who achieved success start benchmarking their wins and their failures and their ways to make big in life and start imposing on the child.

Another child who is born in poverty, hunger has seen parents struggling and fighting for every bit of bread and daily requirements. For them life has been tough and same is being professed in every conversation they have with their children. Children grow up hearing that inculcate the same belief.

Third child who is born in family of artists working in creative fields. They see parents leading individualistic lives following passions and lack of commitment and support to the families. In such cases children tend to have less faith in the institution of marriage etc. which is not a bad thing, but lack of commitment towards your responsibilities is not good either.

Rest of the two or four influencers we choose in life are a matter of emotional, spiritual, intellectual connects. These influencers are chosen by us. Hence process of decision making again becomes relevant.

As the child enters into adolescence, child who has been guided and controlled by first influencers of his / her life, sees that their advice is not yielding results and proving incorrect in lot of situations. His beliefs which he has developed on the basis of the talks and suggestions by first influencer get broken. He starts seeking shelter under next influencer. We as a society do not encourage decision making. At every level free spirit of decision making is discouraged. It's so engrossed in our system to hear the noise and take decisions accordingly that we are incapable of taking decisions at any level.

Even at the highest board level in corporate sector, a group of people come together to take major decisions as the belief is collective decision making is much smarter and prudent. Although past tells us that individual decision makers have made extreme positive impact on World history.

Hence best way to move forward is to remove the fear of What If???? Nobody has conclusive answers of this, apart from Universe and whose help is involved in our process anyways.

One important aspect to ponder at this stage is to understand, how can one achieve this? It's easier said than done to ignore all the advice, all the worldly wisdom and just follow an unknown path.

Let me explain this by using this analogy. There are two kinds of people in this world, people who believe in some form or kind of god or a power beyond us, beyond known to mankind. It can be Jesus or Allah or Shiva or Ram or Gautam Buddha or Krishna or any other temple, church, mosque etc. which gives us power. All these believe their holy books and holy texts are supreme and help one to move forward alighting one from all sorrows and pains. Universally all holy books say that you come and surrender yourself in arms of almighty and he would take care of the rest. Does any holy book preach, that "you hear what others have to say, take their views and opinions and then come to me and I would subsequently show you the path."

 Answer is obviously no.

Then there are other set of people who are atheists and non-conformists and non-believers.

They only have one route and one path. Their Karma and their own ideology. Now for such people automatically not listening to other and not following what others are suggesting is logical. Hence for everyone in this world, common factor remains that all suggestions, all advice given would only deter you from reaching you to right decision and hence the right goal.

Concept of Continuous Affirmation: Most good and bad things happen in this Universe because of this. Rise of ISIL, increase in terrorism, winning of German team in 2014 Football world cup, killing of Osama Bin Laden by US Marines, killing of Saddam Hussein by US, annexing Crimea by Russia is all on account of a single factor.

Imagine you are seated on your desk on Monday morning at 10 AM, and two colleagues come and stand opposite your desk. They talk for a few minutes and end the conversation looking at you and giggling. Both then leave and get back to their seats. Next day the same incident happens. This episode is repeated for a week. Following Monday morning when two of them arrive on your desk and perform the same ritual, you get up from your desk and ask what happened and why are they laughing and why have they been behaving like this. They say we were just sharing some jokes about a man who resembles you. You enquire more about it but they change the topic and move back to their seats.

Next day same thing is repeated. You get angry and wonder if something is funny or weird about you. Do you look funny or have you been dressing badly these days. Also you start exploring what has changed between last 10 days and period prior to that? You get no answers.

Another scenario, you have been working hard all these years and you have been a great performer. For last couple of years, you have been rated highly in your company by your immediate boss. Now one fine day, your boss gives you an assignment. You finish your assignment and hand over the file to your superior. He glances through it and says, "what rubbish is this?" You are wondering, what went wrong and you apologize and take back the file. You check and recheck, everything seems to be in order. You take the file back and your boss tells you to make some minor changes. Again same thing happens for the next assignment and the assignment after that. You start questioning, "Has your work quality deteriorated?" That may not have happened but a person's constant affirmation makes you feel weak and powerless and self-doubts can be created. Each one of us can lower the self-confidence of someone else by simply planting doubts in their mind and then constantly pushing it to make the other person believe that it is the truth or atleast equivalent of truth.

Two world's best tennis players playing on a hot summer in the fifth set are able to outdo each other on

48

the basis of self-affirmation. By the time fifth set sets and body is drained, fatigue has set in but only minds constant affirmation to win helps one to outdo the other.

In a nutshell whenever one is hearing too many noises, too many conversations, too many advices, too many suggestions, too many sermons, too many dialogues, tell yourself "Empty the Sound box within you". Keep saying it a number of times till you are NOT able to hear anyone but you despite of all being around you.

Chapter – 4
R - Refocus on Self. World is Within You

*P*lato said *"The first and best victory is to conquer self.*

To be conquered by self is, of all things, the most shameful & vile".

We believe that everything what happens to us and decisions we take post those events are due to the external world. I would bet, out of eight billion people living on the planet, **at least 7.50 billion people would have blamed once, more or perpetually, acts of others as the reason for the decision taken by them and hence it not working in their favour and hence being a victim of that situation and unable to change it now**.

In a nutshell, we all have a firm belief that what happened with us was not because of us but due to the act of others due which one reacted and have to live through the repercussions of such acts.

My neighbor was driving his car at a high speed on a highway early one morning. Speed limit within city

50

roads is 100 miles/hour and maximum on highways at 140 miles/hr. But seeing empty road he got tempted and started driving at 180 miles/ hour. All of a sudden, a dog jumped and crossed the road, he violently braked and a truck driver driving behind him braked as well. The truck was carrying heavy load and it could not manage the jerk and it fell on the car. In the accident, his wife who was sitting behind in the car died. Fortunately, he and his elder daughter who were sitting in front got away with minor injuries. Now the point here is, if any passerby or anybody who witnessed this accident would blame the truck driver, including my neighbor. But the fact remains, that my neighbor's car was speeding and since the car was speeding, vehicles behind it were also plying at high speed beyond permissible limits, calling for a sure shot eventuality. My final argument is, if the car would have been driven within permissible limits of 140 miles/ hour, even if the truck driver wanted to drive at 180 or 190 miles / hour, he would have honked and my neighbor could have given him the way and moved on one side of the road. This could have prevented the accident and would have saved his wife's life. Most of the time, we believe that whatever output comes in our lives is a matter which is controlled by outside world. At the same time, we want to be the masters of our own destiny. Something is amiss here.

One wants to do things his or her own way and believes that output is not a function of input, but output is dependent on external world.

Isn't this wrong?

What we think, what we do and how we act, repercussions are an after effect of the same.

Content vs Context – One very important fundamental truth we have to follow is the importance of content versus context. What do you mean by Content? Content means what is present in your life. People, things that exist in your life. All materialistic, non-materialistic, emotional, human and non-human lives and things around you form the content.

What is meant by Context- Context means the way you look at a thing, a person, a situation etc.

Most of the time, content of your life is not determined by you. But surely context is. Hence **"If you can't change the content of your life, Change the Context and life would blossom".**

We all have heard several times the age old saying of glass half full versus glass half empty. Context is not only pertaining to a situation, its pertaining to people as well. If your child has dyslexia – a disability to read, write and learn normally. A disorder that involves difficulty in learning to read or interpret words, letters, and other symbols. What are you going to do about it? Child is already four to five years and now you have realized it? Precarious situation. You have few choices.

a. Abandon the child. Leave the child in the orphanage and disown him or her.

b. Keep forcing the child to read and write normally as others by pushing him or her.

c. Keep praying to the almighty for correction and cursing self and the child that why did this happen to him or her.

d. Since the child is slow in learning and can learn only by repetition and once learnt, doesn't get bored of repeating the same act again and again. Would you try and find out what interests the child then let the child learn fine arts, or sports he or she is interested in and make them practice day in day out so that they turn out to be the best.

Most people would initially think of c but eventually under guidance would move to d. So that's what I meant if you can't change the content, change the context and your life would change.

We always have to remember that,

Any opportunity comes only in a disguised form. Its brings misfortune, a bad feeling of disgust, anger, sadness and above all defeat, but which is temporary.

In other words, first a defeat will come, but with your interest, effort and passion, success is inevitable.

We meet so many people in our lives. We deal with so many people in our lives. We interact, we make friends, we fight, we love, we hate, we despise, we respect, we admire, and we feel jealous of people. But who are these people? How did these people come in our lives? Why did it affect me?

The simple answer to this question is – We automatically, universally attract people of our own kind.

Why most business minded people say and share stories of meeting crooks, frauds and people who tried to dupe them. It's exactly from the same reason why you choose to do business with them. Things which were running in your mind when you approached to do business with them or what you did to others comes back to you.

So keep in mind, *what happens to us from outside is nothing but a reflection of what we are from within.*

It's apt to mention here then," What I am, same what I would get".

*Thus it becomes very important to **Find your true You** ?*

In other words if everything which would happen to you or around you is going to present a picture of within you, then it's important to know who you are and need to alter it and change it so that better of you prevails within you.

This would enable better of you to be outside you and hence better for you.

Little confusing, but in a nutshell, find the true goodness in you and same would come for you from the universe. Bring back the focus on you. You have to be on the centrestage and then think about the world around you.

Chapter 5
I - Increase your Bowl

*L*et's start this chapter by asking three simple Questions.

Are you willing to unlearn?

Are you willing to expand your horizons?

Are you willing to pay the price?

Each one of us wishes to be successful, have more money, have more fame, have more friends who praise us and who believe that we are best. But are we ready for it. Are we ready to become big? Most of us dream of becoming king, having princely life but our current actions and our thoughts reflect our pauper mentality. We love a woman who is pretty looking, who is rich, who is snobbish and then we expect her to come to us and say three magical words. How is it possible? Have we increased our horizon? Are we prepared to be in a relationship with her? If you ask anybody that question, he would say yes, I would change when I get it. But, why then? Why not now?

I would use an example here. Do we say first give us good marks then we would study. No you first study hard, and then you expect to get good marks. Similarly, when you practice hard for a game, then you expect to win. Similarly when you prepare yourself to be the winner, successful person, then only your chances or probability to win would increase.

You like that rich beautiful girl, whilst you are poor. What can you do. You are dark and you are short and obviously you are not prince charming. You don't have a Rolls Royce to take her for a drive. You don't have smart clothes. But you have brains. You can learn about her. You can learn about her interests. You can learn what the girl likes. You can learn about the world, its recent events and causes of such events. You can very well analyse cause and effect of each situation. Over and above you can be funny, you can make her laugh. There you go, you are now ready for her. You have increased your bowl, in which she can fit in.

Increase your bowl, means increase your perspective and think beyond. Think as if you have achieved what you are longing for.

ONLY ONE thing which you have been seeking for.

What happens when you achieve that? Plan for next steps even before you have achieved.

It will make you think wider and farther. It would prepare you for the success. Even a mother can't carry the child if her body is not prepared or ready for bringing a new life on this planet.

How can you change your life when you are not prepared to do so?

Think and act and behave as if you have achieved one most important thing that you were working on or person who you have been longing for. It would automatically be yours.

Chapter 6
O - One Big Issue

We all think, as humans, we have great capacity to work, great capacity to execute. We can do the unachievable.

We always follow the simple principle of *"We thought, we conceived, we articulated, we planned, we executed and we achieved"*

It's so simple when you read it. But in actual practice what happens.

We think, and we seek opinions and again we think and we plan, we start and mid-way again we think and again we start something new.

Or some of us we think and we think again it's not right and it can't be done and again we think and just keep thinking.

Science says that average human being uses only 8 to 9 % of his brain capacity. The most intelligent ones move to 14 to 16 %. But is it critical that we use our entire brain. On an average a human being receives 200 thoughts every minute.

We all believe we are great in our work which we do... Yet we don't achieve success. We put out best foot forward, yet we lose. We are good with multitasking and we can finish our work very fast. But sometimes what happens to us, we want to do something very badly. We just want to do it...Now when that kind of feeling comes to us. We share our feelings with our near and dear ones. Most of the time, it is shrugged off as one of our whims and fancies and we move on in our lives. But something in our soul, mind and body in that order is not happy?

Have you come across something like this?

Did you then try and find out, what is bothering you?

Did you think what is of prime importance to you?

We might keep doing our daily job, daily routine, daily chores which our mind and our body is helping to finish but ***Mind can have only one big thought.***

One thought which is troubling you. One thought you wish to convert into action and pursue it.

But is the thought real? Is this thought going to help me in future and if I follow this route, would it bring good to me.

Questions, questions and more questions and finally confusion.

So let's do an exercise, you and me together. Is your thought real and is your thought achievable. Before that we have to believe this is tangible and you can conquer it.

So let's articulate it and frame it in a sentence or a cluster or words.

Example "I wish to earn USD 5 million by 2020".

"I wish to win an Olympic gold medal by 2025."

"I wish to join London School of economics through full scholarship program by 2018"

After you have articulated your thought, let's do a mind exercise.

Let mind go for a virtual walk. Next steps are simple. Slide into your seat, couch and be in a comfortable dreamy position in which you can take a power nap.

Don't worry, you are not going to sleep. You are going into the state of trance.

Close your eyes. Take four deep breaths of 2 seconds each. For simplicity sake count each second. Each second would determine inhalation and exhalation. Now see your each body part with your eyes closed from head to toe.

Now imagine you are leaving your body. You are now standing next to your body. Leave your body here and move on. Let the dream which you have framed earlier during the exercise, hit your mind. Can you see it clearly?

What happen after achieving that goal or destination?

After you have achieved you goal, who all form part of your life. How is your life changing after achieving your goal? How has your life transformed now?

Is it only your immediate family getting benefitted from this accomplishment? Or after your goal is achieved, the world at large and Universe at large figures as a part of your success and getting something out of you from your accomplishment.

In between this act, too many thoughts are striking you but your life is clear and you have visualized it as if it's happening to you now.

Just stay with this thought and open your eyes to move to the next step.

Chapter 7
U- Us Vs Them – Spirit of Oneness

Each one of us have two sides obviously one good side and one not so good side. Not necessarily a bad side. So sometimes, we are extremely concerned about people around us, people whom we don't know, people whom we have no connection apart from they just being co humans. But we feel for them. We read about them, we see them in documentaries; we hear about them and feel like doing something for them.

But then our not so good side emerges and it tells us let me focus on myself, my family at best and if possible my folks. Or my friends can also be included in the list. But generally to gain something for me or for the list mentioned above, I would not essentially harm anybody. So I gain but with no loss to others.

Some of us who have gone through lot of pain, lot of suffering would think that as long as I 'm gaining, I really don't care what happens to the world. Now that's not a bad thing to feel. It's fine you have decided to be selfish and be self-centered. Mostly you would also achieve what you have been struggling for. In most of the cases it would be money and only money and that's it. But still you would be not be happy and would remain directionless. As you have earned money and more money and you have harmed millions of people in the process. If not millions, atleast a few and what goes around comes back to you for sure. So you would be running again because of some illness, some litigation, some natural calamity or family feud and it would be a journey that would not allow you rest and would not allow you to be " *What you are and what you want to be* " and would keep taking away gradually what you have acquired through the years.

Hence it's important that you are not in third situation, as this process might be of no use as it would not yield result , when you intend or thinking of harming something or somebody and forcing to shift the equilibrium of the Universe. So it's important that you fall in first two categories. Good and not so good.

You would be thinking how difficult is to change once you are in 3rd situation of being bad or 2nd situation of not being so good.

Just try and answer two below questions - *Is it only about me or would it later include the world at large?*

Do I want to satisfy my Insatiable Ego and its fulfillment?

If answer is No, you have already moved in the first space. But if answer to any of the queries if yes, then keep moderating your statement, keep altering it till answer becomes no and that when you are there.

Keep that statement with you and don't leave it. It's ok if you don't have a wish or statement or something to work on. You might just have a problem, in hand. Great we would find answers. Keep it with you.

Chapter 8
M - My Anxiety Vs My Desire

A step forward in decision making is to figure out, how badly you want the effects of the decision you have taken to be fructified. In other words the change in path or attainment of higher speed on the same path resulting out of the decision taken by you.

As per the Oxford dictionary desire is defined as, "a strong feeling of wanting to have something or wishing for something to happen"

Whilst it's interesting to note that anxiety has two undertones. People believe anxiety to be highly negative which the first statement of Oxford dictionary shows.

It states anxiety as, "a feeling of worry, nervousness, or unease about something with an uncertain outcome."

This statement reflects that one who desires feels worried of the end result. An act or decision taken in the past which would have implications. Also it shows that things or actions which you have not done or taken and which are beyond your control, worries about them.

When Lehman went bust, some of the highly paid bond traders were sacked and post the Bear Sterns crisis and before Lehman went bust in Sept 2008, there were anxious days. But is it really anxiety? What could the Lehman employees do, perhaps the few at management level could look for a suitor but a newly employed Ivy school graduate who joined Lehman surely would not have been instrumental in changing the outcome.

Then why get anxious. It comes again to third chapter of the book. If you can't change the content, change the context. You have thought of earning a seven digit USD salary, fair but move on and hunt for smart bargains in US or shift to emerging markets for the time being.

Then there is another definition of *Anxiety,* "

Strong desire or concern to do something or for something to happen".

Now that's what I refer as need. When a thing, a motive, a thought becomes obsession and desire no longer remains a desire but something which you can't live without, that is the decision of your lifetime.

In next two chapters you would actually practice the art of decision making, idea generation, evolution of choices etc.

Chapter 9
P - Potty Pot Prognosis

*I*n this entire book, we have been trying to discuss

your life, your experiences, your success, and your decisions. But when have you been with yourself last. All alone, just you and with you, only. Are you thinking? Still thinking… Perhaps….

Most of us wants best for us and then have no time for us only.

Isn't it funny? We want so much from our lives and don't want to give time to our lives.

But I guess you are wrong? You are giving time to yourself daily. Or rather Universe has scheduled time for you to be with you. When is it?

It's when you are removing the unwanted stuff from your body through the means of excreta. This is the Potty time. Time when you are all alone, time when you are not bothered what's happening to the outside world and outside world doesn't care what you are doing inside.

Potty or excretion is a process by which you are not only creating space in your stomach and cleaning your digestive system but also creating space in your mental system.

Space essential for new ideas to be born.

New ray of hope to enter your life. New method, new means to do something better or something similar in a better way.

We don't realize when we throw excreta out of human system, our negative thoughts, negative vibes and negative approach all gets out of us. We go out and again get entangled every day and then come back to clean our system again. We don't realize the time which we spend during potty is the most useful two minutes to sixty minutes of our daily lives.

We sometimes pollute it by taking worldly pollution inside our toilets in the form of newspaper, mobile phones, laptops etc. and try and read stuff. During that time when space is naturally created in our system and most importantly in our minds, it's getting blocked out by information thrown by gadgets and print. During the process of excretion, Universe sees space and radiates and transmits fresh opportunities and signals, which come to us in the form of new purpose, target, thoughts etc.

During these two minute to sixty minute, when we are a free spirit, nobody to judge, nobody to be answerable to, nobody to be bothered about, We experience our liberated soul. Thus in the free spirit, alternatives, choices, possibilities emerge in front of us.

Critical thing to note here is that, during this small window of two minutes to sixty minutes (depending how much time individual spends on Potty Pot), our receptive brain network is very active and hence it moves very fast receiving multiple ideas and multiple choices. Key thing is to swiftly narrow down to limited number of alternatives and make a mental note of those possibilities. In this part of the process, Universe only brings thoughts and hence decision making process is yet not over, which would align you with the Universal plan of success.

To practice this part, tomorrow when you would enter your toilet and sit on your potty pot, carry your problem, take it along with you, but one major issue, one big challenge which you are not able to crack. One thing, which has been bothering you constantly. But don't carry any props or reading material whilst you are inside the loo. You would witness nothing short of magic in the form of possibilities emerging in front of you, options which you never have dreamt would come alive in front of you.

Let's take a deeper dive in this process of Potty Pot Prognosis.

Two simple questions, which would come in your mind automatically

1. Why should I sit on pot or why do you say that ideation process would be successful on pot?

2. What is the source of these ideas?

Answer to first one is you can sit on pot or on any other thing or at any other place. But the process of excretion helps you relieve not only your body but your mind. We keep feeding our body with good & bad (food/ water / other elements), but body only extracts useful component of it and throws away rest of the unwanted stuff through the process of excretion. When body does that, mind also clears up its excreta and relieves it. When space is created in the body, mind is prepared as well to generate and absorb and originate fresh ideas.

73

Answer to second question is fairly simple. We get ideas from two sources, One from our past experiences and learnings and second from Universe.

Now imagine if these ideas coincide with your mind, heart, body and past experience and Universe as well gives you green signal, then success is a surety than a probability. But how do your ideas and next steps fit you fit in the Universal plan. To understand that let's read the final chapter of this book.

Chapter 10
H - Hot Head Bath Test

This chapter would aid you to decide and choose from the various alternatives which were just presented to you in the last chapter. In case you have only one feasible choice then this process would lead you to take a deeper dive on that possibility and would enable you to have next action points. Constructive execution detail with next steps would emerge in front of you.

Water, as we all know is extremely important for our survival. One can live without food for almost thirty days, but without water, it's difficult to survive for more than thirty six to forty eight hours. So the last and most important phase which would guide you to your life changing decision is the Hot Head Bath test. You must be wondering, I take hot water bath every day and nothing has changed in my life for so many years and now Rastogi Siddhartha is telling me to do this again and my life would change.

Answer is YES.

During olden times, bathrooms used to be as big as or even bigger than the rooms people lived in. Most of the important thinking and introspection used to happen in bathrooms. Where bathrooms ceased to exist, people used to spend time near the flowing water of the river. Flowing water or moving water represents life. Life which exists and life which is progressing. Nonstop movement of water thus can assist us in our next journey.

I'm sure we all have taken hot water baths. Mostly hot water baths are taken in colder regions for obvious reasons and generally pre or post bath are important events. Have you thought why your mind tells you to have a hot water bath, so that all doubts, all confusion is cleared post the bath and you feel rejuvenated?

After a tiring day at work or after playing a tiring match, you would want your energy to come back and that's what hot water bath does to you.

Have you also felt during hot water bath; you feel completely drained out, energy less with no power and no strength. Why does that happen and how is that linked to great decision making. Continuous flow of hot water cuts the flow of energy in the Universe. It delinks your body and mind from all connections and hence you would be away from all sources of positive and negative vibrations and that's why you feel little low. But actually what's happening is, choices which have appeared for you are moving away as your biases are. Only the one which would mean good for you and beneficial from Universal perspective for you and for the world at large would remain. Also as old and carried forward ways and notions die, new actionable start to blossom giving you clear path to move on.

The learning of this book would be completely futile, if one doesn't implement the thought which has come out of the process. Constant thinking and procrastination of thoughts, thinking about the worldly excuses would make this exercise redundant. Speed of execution would determine the success of the thought and plan which has evolved out of the process.

Final destination from this process would lead you to have an Inner Transformation. A change.

Which would come in you as a part of following constant process as has been outlined above.

After a few times of trial your body and mind are attuned to this activity and effortlessly you will move.

In the same path as Universe would take you being the means and not the end.

When I learnt this art of decision making (calling it art as conclusion as almost everything, about decision making is invisible and can't be judged or activated by numbers or facts), first thing I did was to disperse this information through this book to each one of you.

My belief that this book is a part of the larger Universal program or plan which would aid and help millions and would find it path and cover the journey to reach the one who in turn is part Of the larger plan beyond self-aiding and changing the world altogether.

I can challenge through this book, that if anybody who is about to take extreme step of killing somebody or committing suicide, or harming someone else follows the eight minute process or even the last two steps of the process, would change his /her mind. This book would provide direction to everyone who is confused with multiple options or with NO OPTION.

This book would open a window of opportunity, a ray of light through which you can decide the path and move forward for a constructive and successful future.

Final line from my side – Get your biggest problem or answers you have been looking for a while, carry is with you tomorrow morning, try the process, get options, make the decision and execute with the speed of light. Life outside is waiting for your successful and glorious future.

Concluding words

You must be feeling little amazed, little foolish, and little happy all at the same time. Little amazed since this is such a simple process, which you execute everyday but never bothered to gain or benefit out of it. Little foolish that an author some miles away has to tell you about this simple process. And finally happy because now you know about this simple yet unique process of finding answers to all your problems and queries.

One request from my end to each one of you who is reading this book in any format. Kindly give reviews, views, comments, thoughts, bad words, good words, appreciation, criticism but communicate to me and communicate to millions who would read this book or not read this book. Please write at: 8minutedecision@gmail.com

How would it help???

It you think its good; your views would enable others to read.

If you think this book is not worthwhile and not helpful then, ensure that rest of the world who is not exposed to the book do not waste their time.

www.ingramcontent.com/pod-product-compliance
Lightning Source LLC
Chambersburg PA
CBHW060532030426
42337CB00021B/4218